THE BUSINESS MODEL CANVAS

Let your business thrive with this simple model

Written by Magali Marbaise
Translated by Carly Probert

50MINUTES.com

PROPEL YOUR BUSINESS FORWARD!

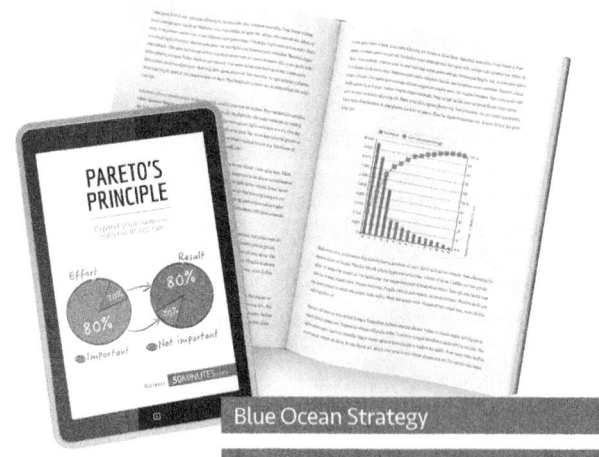

- Blue Ocean Strategy
- Pareto's Principle
- Managing Stress at Work
- Game Theory

www.50minutes.com

THE BUSINESS MODEL CANVAS — 1

Key information
Introduction
Definition of the model

THEORY — 4

The nine tools

PRACTICAL APPLICATION — 11

Tips and best practices
Case study

LIMITATIONS AND EXTENSIONS — 21

Limitations and criticisms
Related models and extensions

SUMMARY — 25

FURTHER READING — 28

THE BUSINESS MODEL CANVAS

KEY INFORMATION

- **Name:** Business Model Canvas, BMC.
- **Uses:** The Business Model Canvas is a valuable strategic tool which is used to conceptualise new business models or to document existing ones. It helps to guide decisions about the launch of a product, a startup or a new process by illustrating the value and core activity of a company.
- **Why is it successful?** The simplicity and clarity of the tool's visual presentation make it easy to use alone or as part of a team.
- **Key words:**
  - Business model: The model through which a company creates value. Through a strategy for developing the core business, this value should manifest itself in financial rewards for companies that are able to satisfy their customers.
  - Business plan: A projection, written down in an official document, which outlines this strategy based on market analyses and rigorously gathered and studied data.
  - Canvas: A basic outline which groups together a collection of elements in a structured way.

INTRODUCTION

Ambitious employees who want to rise through the ranks in their company and make revolutionary, high-value ideas viable, as well as entrepreneurs who want to reinvigorate their company or increase their market share, would benefit from gaining an in-depth understanding of how their business works, how it generates growth and which growth levers are the most useful. The Business Model Canvas is an excellent way of developing this understanding.

This strategic tool was developed by Alexander Osterwalder (Austrian theorist, born in 1974) and Yves Pigneur (Belgian computer scientist and professor at the University of Lausanne, born in 1954) in their bestselling book *Business Model Generation* (2010). It is used mainly (though not exclusively) by entrepreneurs, and aims to enable them to transform their ideas into innovative and competitive projects. To do this, the authors encourage every company that uses the Business Model Canvas to reflect on the value that they create for their customers and for themselves. This model is particularly suited to those operating in small businesses or startups, where the structure is not strongly hierarchical: the canvas offers a more systematic approach than the majority of traditional models by articulating the different component parts of the business.

DEFINITION OF THE MODEL

According to the creators of the method, this framework allows organisations to create, deliver and capture value (Osterwalder and Pigneur, 2010).

The Business Model Canvas is part of the visual and design thinking trend. This means that, through its non-linear process, it enables the creation of a visual system that is accessible, readable and easy to understand for everybody. This canvas is a medium which entrepreneurs can use to reflect on and construct their business model on a single page: they can easily organise their ideas in the boxes in the template, in order to move more quickly – and effectively – to action. The fact that it offers an overview of the models under construction facilitates the clear definition of priorities, the creation of concrete action plans and a creative and adaptable approach, which greatly simplifies the future development of a business plan. This tool also improves interactions with customers and boosts communication between employees.

THEORY

All companies dream of holding the keys to success, and the simpler they are, the better! Although this framework does not really take into account the purely competitive aspect, it is still very interesting, practical and accessible to all.

THE NINE TOOLS

The matrix consists of nine interrelated blocks that illustrate all the activities of a company:

- key activities
- key partnerships
- key resources
- customer segments
- channels
- customer relationships
- value proposition
- cost structure
- revenue streams.

Clearly differentiated and identified, the boxes are carefully and precisely arranged on the canvas. This layout creates synergies between them, resulting in a unique strategy for every company that tries the exercise.

	Key activities		Customer relationships	
Key partnerships		Value proposition		Customer segments
	Key resources		Channels	
Cost structure			Revenue streams	

Creating value

	Key activities		Customer relationships	
Key partnerships		Value proposition		Customer segments
	Key resources		Channels	
Cost structure			Revenue streams	

- **Key activities.** The key activities are essential to the company, since a customer value proposition is created through them, which indirectly generates income. These activities vary, depending on the type of business model. For example, in an insurance company, a key activity is

protecting client assets and compensating them in case of loss; a hospital will be responsible for the health of patients. According to Osterwalder, the activities can be classified in three different categories:
- Those directly related to the manufacturing of a product;
- Those seeking to develop solutions (services) to meet customer needs;
- Those that take place, in whole or in part, on the internet (online shopping sites or banks).

- **Key partnerships.** The saying "two heads are better than one" is universal and has particular resonance in the professional world, within our companies. Having and maintaining good relationships with carefully selected, competitive and reliable partners strengthens the position occupied by the organisation within its market by reinforcing the business model. The nature of the partnership depends on the company's aims:
  - Subcontracting to foster economies of scale or refocus activities;
  - Mergers to reduce the risk and uncertainty linked to the competitive environment;
  - Acquisition of certain resources and activities which allows some activities to be outsources to other companies. An example of this would be an insurance company that uses an external assessment office to pay claims.

There are various key partner profiles. Whether the partner is a company or an individual, the important thing is that they provide support, advice, etc., which

will facilitate the development of a company: banks, investors, associates, suppliers or even customers, but also competitors.
- **Key resources.** These are the company's assets, which it relies on and which enable it to maintain its economic activity or successfully carry out its value chain. There is therefore a degree of interdependence between the health of the company – both financial and human, intellectual (patents, etc.) or material – and the resources available for (re)launching a value proposition. Following this logic, small and medium size businesses will make the most of the relatively small size of their teams (human resources) to focus on regular personal contact with clients. Conversely, an IT company may prefer to focus on material resources such as processors, coolers or warehouses in order to enhance its value proposition.
- **Customer segments.** The majority of companies owe their prosperity to their customers, who are the driving force behind many economic activities. It is therefore important to know them well, to identify their expectations and to propose an offer that best meets their needs. From these, the organisation establishes customer segments with the same or similar needs and chooses which groups to target in particular.

DEFINING AND CHOOSING SEGMENTS

There are different types of customer segments, such as the mass market, the niche market, the diversified market, etc. Depending on the type of activity chosen, its financial capacity and the economic situation, the company will target one segment or another. For example, an upscale restaurant will seek to attract mainly affluent customers, while a brasserie will offer a more affordable menu (unless it is willing to offer something different and aim for a different kind of clientele; in that case, it will opt for a different approach, for example by offering higher-quality wines and emphasising this choice in its communications). The choice of segment can also be based on geographical location: the establishment of a high-end restaurant seems more appropriate in some places than others (in the town centre or in the countryside).

- **Channels.**
  - Value propositions are delivered to customers through channels. Advertising, social networks, etc. are crucial 'interfaces' between the company and its customers.
- **Customer relationships.** The optimisation of customer relationships is a favourite topic for any company. Nurturing relationships with the consumers of value propositions encourages their loyalty, thus guaranteeing in a way the sustainability of the company. A relationship is built through repeated contact between the customer and the product/service/business, whether this involves consumption or experience as such, or exposure to the marketing around the offer. Each company must therefore establish a concrete policy by which it defines its current and future customer relationships. These relationships can take several forms, including a more personalised approach, self-service and standardisation.

- **Value proposition.** Value propositions are the services or products that the company offers (sells) to its customers.

> **WHAT IS VALUE?**
>
> Value is what allows a company to expand and to win over and retain customers looking for added value: value for money, brand, quality of service and efficiency. In order to realise this value, it is therefore important to know which needs have been met – and, above all, which needs have not been met – on the market, and to analyse what is being offered by the competition.

Financial equilibrium

Key partnerships	Key activities	Value proposition	Customer relationships	Customer segments
	Key resources		Channels	
Cost structure				Revenue streams

- **Cost structure.** Many parts of the business model incur and generate costs (advertising is a good example).
- **Revenue streams.** This box will contain the answers

to the following questions: What are the sources of revenue? What price are customers willing to pay and for what products? Generating revenue streams is therefore crucial, since the survival of any business depends on it. The most common offers include the sale of goods, right of use (customers pay to use the product or service), subscriptions, leases/loans, etc. Beyond this income from the B2C relationship, revenue from B2B partnerships, such as advertising and sponsorship, must not be neglected.

PRACTICAL APPLICATION

TIPS AND BEST PRACTICES

Organising a BMC workshop

As mentioned previously, this model is interactive: participants from the company sit down, draw the matrix on a large sheet of paper, which they stick up on a wall or place in the middle of the table, discuss, interact and 'stick' their ideas on the model. The Post-it® method, suggested by Osterwalder, appears very effective in the context of this groupwork: ideas can be removed, replaced and moved as the discussion progresses and different points are made. During the workshop, the Business Model Canvas does not remain 'fixed', but rather is built up one Post-it® Note at a time (Osterwalder and Pigneur, 2010), since:

- Users actively think about what they should place in each box in the model by asking themselves a series of questions. For example, for the value proposition, it would be interesting to think about the value the company provides for the customer, the problem they propose to resolve, the needs they are responding to, etc. These points should be tackled in as much depth as possible.
- Each participant has a pad of sticky notes and a pen, which allows them to share their thoughts with their colleagues and organise their ideas at the same time. In this approach, the business model is developed by brainstorming and jotting down ideas. The main idea is that simplicity stimulates creativity. The aim is also to

involve employees at all levels of the company.

Finally, companies must remember to test their model regularly. Putting forward hypotheses allows the business model to be fine-tuned as the company develops.

RECOMMENDATIONS FROM THE AUTHORS

To create and implement a new business model, Osterwalder and Pigneur suggest working in five phases:

- **Mobilising** by defining the precise aims of the project, testing the first ideas, planning the project and putting together a team of experienced and enthusiastic people with different profiles;
- **Understanding**, through market research and cross-sectional analyses;
- **Designing**, which involves exploring, testing and letting go of preconceived ideas that are comforting, but which prevent people from seeing things differently;
- **Creating** by implementing a business plan and a financial plan;
- **Managing** by rigorously monitoring the situation on a day-to-day basis in order to adjust or even possibly rethink the business model.

Quick recommendations

When a leader is considering rethinking the business model of their company, they should always:

- ensure that their approach is legitimate, relevant and consistent;
- provide for the active participation of all levels of the company in order to obtain a comprehensive overview and avoid possible resistance to change;
- call in an impartial mediator who can lead the discussions and challenge participants;
- take stock of what already exists in order to decide whether to start from scratch or not;
- decide who to put in charge of the project to ensure a smooth transition when implementing new guidelines.

CASE STUDY

This case study takes as its subject a non-specialised bookstore, which sells novels, books on art and music, academic books and scientific books. It is renowned for the quality of its recommendations on literature, as well as for its large catalogue of school and university textbooks.

As the book sector has undergone many changes in recent years, such as the introduction of online sales, bookstores are becoming less and less busy. In addition, the outlet in question is facing tough competition: there are several bookstores in a small area, and each of them is trying to get ahead by diversifying or specialising. Specifically, a direct competitor has emerged in the market for school books. It is therefore time for the store to reconsider its business model in order to remain open.

The manager of the bookstore decides to review his business model and calls together his staff (the communication team, the accountant, booksellers, the reception team, etc.) to review the situation. Together, they must ask a series of questions in order to fill in the canvas and update the current business model. It is important to note here that they can start with any square on the model.

Advice for leaders

Osterwalder warns against some pitfalls:

- Do not be afraid of overly bold ideas, to the point of systematically rejecting them. Although they may generate more risks, they are also often more interesting. However, this does not mean approving them with no further reflection. For example, they can be tested initially, then adjusted and adapted if they prove effective.
- Do not automatically start from scratch, because there may be some useful elements to retain from the previous model.
- Do not exclude certain team members, because the best ideas often emerge through sharing.
- Do not focus only on the short term. As with any business model design, looking at the long term limits risks.

Analysis of the old business model

As the discussions progress, the canvas fills up and reveals an overview of the current state of affairs, with the strengths and weaknesses of the current business model.

Key partnerships	Key activities	Value proposition	Customer relationships	Customer segments
• Suppliers/ distributors	• Providing quality advice • Constant optimisation (market research, etc.)	• Advice • Competitive prices	• Confidence • Reliability • Adapted to customer	• Universities • Libraries • Loyal customers • Regular customers
	Key resources • Human resources • Finances and cash flow		**Channels** • Mail/telephone • Direct contact	

Cost structure	Revenue stream
Orders from suppliers: variable costs according to the volume of books ordered and discounts granted.	Direct sales of goods (payment at the till or by invoice)

Business Model Canvas © 50MINUTES.com

- **Customer segments. Who are the biggest customers of the bookstore? What segments are reached? Who do they create value for?** In this case, the main customers come from schools and universities, which directly send their students to this bookstore. Libraries and loyal customers – mostly pensioners – regularly visit to benefit from its recommendations.
  ○ Steady market: Libraries and loyal customers.
  ○ Market to recapture each year: universities.

- Visits from individuals or the general public, who know the name of the bookstore or have already visited, and who come once or more per year, at more or less random times (specific book or order, browsing, gifts, etc.).
- **Value proposition. What is the added value of the bookstore?**
    - Wise advice for loyal customers, the public and librarians.
    - 'Unbeatable prices' for some librarians and for schools or universities (and therefore indirectly for students).
- **Channels. How does the store communicate with customers? What channels does it use?** The channels currently used are essentially email and telephone. Universities and libraries are generally contacted remotely, while booksellers work through direct contact with customers who visit the store.
- **Customer relationships. What kind of relationships does the bookstore have with its customers?** It maintains a relationship of trust with loyal customers, and with institutions such as libraries and universities. In these relationships, everyone benefits: the company can reduce its costs, while libraries and universities purchase their books at the best price. The customer relationship is adapted depending on the client.
- **Revenue streams. What do the customers pay for? How do they pay?** Goods are sold directly: customers pay directly at the counter or by invoice for libraries and universities. They pay with the knowledge that they are receiving a service and advice that they are accustomed to and appreciate.

- **Key resources. What key resources does the bookstore's value proposition require?**
  - The key resources of a bookstore are primarily human resources, especially nowadays. Customers go there to receive advice and maintain a special relationship with the bookseller.
  - The second key resource is financial (sale prices and discounts discussed suppliers, who have a particular impact on sales to universities and libraries).
- **Key activities. What are the key activities resulting from the value proposition of the bookstore?** In order to ensure the best price for universities and libraries, the manager does regular market research on the prices and services offered by the competition. Moreover, the quality of the advice depends on the expertise of the booksellers.
- **Key partnerships. Who are the bookstore's key partners? Who does it work with? Which partners help it to create value?** The bookshop has established reliable relationships with a network of specialised suppliers. Their economic situations are closely linked: a decline in sales for the bookstore results in a loss of income for the suppliers. The suppliers have therefore drawn up a list of orders that should be reviewed regularly, as they do not always correspond to the actual bookstore sales (surplus books that the store does not manage to sell). A balance must therefore be found, especially since some suppliers 'block' orders if the bookstore is in arrears with its payments (this of course implies less stock, which in turn generates fewer sales, thus creating a vicious circle). It is therefore vital to maintain a relationship of trust with

suppliers. Distributors also play a major role, because it is imperative that the bookstore meets its promised delivery times. In this respect, competition is tough with websites that guarantee delivery within two to three working days. This point can be improved upon, since the bookstore is currently suffering from long delays.
- **Cost structure. What are the main costs of the bookstore? What are the most expensive activities?** The booksellers handle orders directly. The manager handles specific requests from universities in order to order larger quantities. Purchase costs vary, because they depend on the volume of orders and any discounts offered by the supplier: they are currently too high. Salary costs are also significant, because the average age of employees is relatively high.

Adaptation of the business model

When the participants, anything seems possible: they simply have to dare to ask the questions necessary to update the business model. They can begin their reflection with any of the boxes on the canvas. Ideally, they should ensure that innovations are imagined for each box of the canvas and then choose the most suitable suggestion for the situation.

Thus, by adding, removing, and moving the sticky notes with the various ideas of each bookstore employee, the model is represented more objectively, which generates new constructive synergies.

Major changes:

Key partnerships	Key activities	Value proposition	Customer relationships	Customer segments
• Partnership with other bookstores • New distributor for better delivery times • Improve contact with suppliers	• Providing quality advice • Constant optimisation (market research, etc.) • Reading workshops • Partnership development	• Quality of customer advice • Different and competitive offer	• Confidence • Reliability • Offer adapted to customer • Personal management	• Universities • Libraries • Loyal customers • Regular customers • Schools, professors, students • Reduced mobility customers or those who can no longer travel
	Key resources • Human resources • Finances • Employee training to develop new activities • Quality website (online orders)		**Channels** • Mail/telephone • Clearer communication • Direct contact • Internet (website)	

Cost structure	Revenue Stream
Orders from suppliers: variable costs according to the volume of books ordered → Reduction of costs	Direct sales of goods (payment at the till or by invoice) → Increased revenue

This new version of the business model places the customer at the heart of its concerns: it seeks to optimise the value proposition, develop customer relationships, etc. This last dimension, which is often overlooked or put to one side by companies, can intelligently guide strategic choices. The new configuration is more responsive to the problems faced by the bookstore, because the customer, who may have different reasons for reading (from the loyal, older customer to the development of a new segment which is younger and/or no longer travels to the bookstore) is placed at the centre of the economic structure. The bookstore primarily needs to review its key activities (readings, literary events, employee training), its cost structure (website, salary costs), its key partners (distributors, suppliers, competitors), its communication channels (development of its website), etc.

LIMITATIONS AND EXTENSIONS

LIMITATIONS AND CRITICISMS

- **Lack of focus on the strategic aspect.** As outlined previously, the BMC ignores the strategic aspect of the business. It places the value proposition at the centre of its approach, assuming that the primary desire of any business is to make money. This is significant, if not essential, for the survival of companies, but not all of them put profits at the top of their agenda. In particular, this is the case for non-profit associations. The strategic approach is important for the development of any company, and by disregarding it we risk missing out on important customer segments that we perhaps had not considered.
- **Cannot be applied to all companies.** According to Philippe Moricou (Professor of Strategy at the ESSCA) in an interview with the site My-Business-Plan.fr, it would appear that the BMC can be applied more easily to single activity companies, such as startups, than to multidisciplinary organisations. Moricou believes that this is due to the simplicity of the matrix. Indeed, the potential synergies between the different activities may not necessarily fit into the relatively basic boxes in the model.
- **Failure to consider the competition.** The Business Model Canvas focuses on the structure and inner workings of the company, and does not take into account (or only considers to a very limited extent) external factors, such as competition. However, thinking about competition when establishing the model is important,

as a change on this level may have a direct effect on it, by requiring the company to revise its targets, for example. In our case study, the company wanted to review its business model due to increasing competition that risked affecting its value propositions.
- **Static analysis.** The BMC does not account for the evolution of the business under study: it allows for an overview of the situation at a given time and therefore completely ignores the long-term view.

RELATED MODELS AND EXTENSIONS

As the Business Model Canvas has some limitations, including in particular the lack of a strategic dimension, it is worth considering combining it with other tools so that they can complement one another.

The BCG matrix to guide strategy

The BCG matrix for strategic management

Based on the four types of strategic business areas (stars, question marks, cash cows and dogs), this model can complement the BMC, which does not take into account these realities that influence strategic choices. The idea of the BCG matrix is to evaluate both the market of the product and the growth prospects of the product in the market. The company uses these parameters to determine priorities in its product portfolio and ensure long-term value creation and the management of cash flow.

Porter's Five Forces to beat the competition

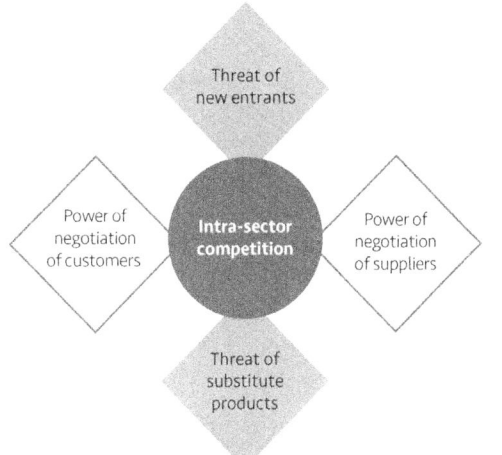

Porter's Five Forces determine the attractiveness of an industry. The assumption is that companies seek a competitive advantage that is measured by their ability to generate profits or to capture resources. These five forces are: potential entrants (those who can enter the market and be a threat), substitute products (products in direct competition), customers and distributors, as well as suppliers (who all have bargaining power).

SUMMARY

- The Business Model Canvas comes from the book *Business Model Generation: A Handbook for Visionaries, Game Changers and Challengers*, co-written by Alexander Osterwalder and Yves Pigneur in 2011.
- It is a practical model, which is very easy to use and directly applicable. It involves all levels in the company hierarchy, but is more suitable for startups than large businesses.
- The matrix is based on the value proposition provided to customers. The nine blocks that make up the canvas overlap, and the business model is developed using the synergies created between them:
    - key activities
    - key partnerships
    - key resources
    - customer segments
    - channels
    - customer relationships
    - value proposition
    - cost structure
    - revenue streams.
- The use of sticky notes stimulates creativity because they can be freely moved around during a workshop. This involves the different participants who are reflecting on the company's value creation. The goal is to be aware of the various measures that need to be put in place in order to implement a concrete and directly applicable plan.
- The authors make several important recommendations:

ensure the legitimacy of the process, emphasise an overview of the model, consider a mediator to lead discussions, take stock of the current situation, and identify the people responsible for the realisation of the project.
- As we have seen in the concrete example of the bookstore, customer relationships and value propositions are fundamental in this canvas. However, the authors warn business leaders to not be afraid of being too inventive, to involve as many people as possible in the design of the BMC, and to take what they already know as their starting point rather than beginning again from scratch, as this could cause serious problems with consistency.
- This tool does nonetheless have some limitations, such as its failure to cover strategic and competitive aspects. Using it alongside a business plan will ensure that no detail is forgotten.

*We want to hear from you!
Leave a comment on your online library
and share your favourite books on social media!*

FURTHER READING

BIBLIOGRAPHY

- Créativité.net (2016) *Business Model – Nouvelle Génération: Un guide pour visionnaires, révolutionnaires et challengers d'Alexander Osterwalder et d'Yves Pigneur.* [Online]. [Accessed 20 July 2015]. Available from: <http://www.creativite.net/business-model-nouvelle-generation-alexander-osterwalder-yves-pigneur/>
- Kotler, P., Keller, K. and Manceau, D. (2012) *Marketing Management.* 14th edition. Paris: Pearson.
- Menin-Urien, G. (2012) 2013, action commercial – Conseil 6 : apportez de la valeur ajoutée! *Le Blog du Manager commercial.* [Online]. [Accessed 20 July 2015]. Available from: <http://www.management-commercial.fr/2012/12/21/2013-quelle-action-commerciale-apportez-de-la-valeur-ajoutee/>
- My-Business-Plan.fr (2013) *Philippe Mouricou vous dit tout sur le Business Model Nouvelle Génération.* [Online] [Accessed 8 July 2015]. Available from: <http://www.my-business-plan.fr/interview-philippe-mouricou-business-model>
- Osterwalder, A. and Pigneur, Y. (2010) *Business Model Generation: A Handbook for Visionaries, Game Changers, and Challengers.* Hoboken, New Jersey: John Wiley & Sons.
- UCM (2016) *Le Business Model Canvas. Un outil stratégique pour l'entreprise.* [Online]. [Accessed 8 July 2015]. Available from: <http://www.ucm.be/Entreprendre/Le-Business-Model-Canvas-Un-outil-strategique-pour-l-

entreprise>
- University of Lausanne. (2016) Yves Pigneur. *Facultés des Hautes Études Commerciales*. [Online]. [Accessed 20 July 2015]. Available from: <https://hec.unil.ch/people/ypigneur>

ADDITIONAL SOURCES

- Business Model Canvas website: http://www.businessmodelgeneration.com/canvas/bmc
- Alexander Osterwalder website: http://alexosterwalder.com/

VIDEOS

- *Business Model Canvas Explained*. (2011) [Video]. Available from: <https://youtu.be/QoAOzMTLP5s>
- *Osterwalder explaining the Business Model Canvas*. (2012) [Video]. Available from: <https://www.youtube.com/watch?v=RzkdJiax6Tw>

WOULD YOU LIKE TO LEARN EVEN MORE?

Would you like to talk to Alexander Osterwalder on Twitter? Are you interested in taking his online course or even hiring him as a speaker? All of this is possible! Find out more on his website.

Although the editor makes every effort to verify the accuracy of the information published, 50Minutes.com accepts no responsibility for the content of this book.

© 50MINUTES.com, 2016. All rights reserved.

www.50minutes.com

Ebook EAN: 9782806279378

Paperback EAN: 9782806285881

Legal Deposit: D/2016/12603/524

Cover: © Primento

Digital conception by Primento, the digital partner of publishers.